When One Song Ends

Birdsong, Barks, and Banter II

Shirl Knobloch

When One Song Ends: Birdsong, Barks, and Banter II

Edited by: Jennifer Sabatelli

Cover and Photography by: Shirl Knobloch

ISBN 13: 979-8-218-04233-2

Also By Shirl Knobloch:

Birdsong, Barks, and Banter: Adventures of an Animal Intuitive Reiki Master and Her Home of Misfit Companions

The Returning Ones: A Medium's Memoirs

You're Never Too Old for Fairy Tales

Reenactments from My Heart: Spiritual and Supernatural Civil War Fiction and Poetry

Once Upon a Fairy Tale

Strength of a Lion, Soul of a Lamb: A Collection of Wolfhound Fairy Tales and Poetry

My Ten Legged Journey: The Road to Rainbow Bridge

Waiting for the Next Village Attack: Growing Up Italian, a Jersey Girl Reminisces

Enchanted: Fairy Tales for Old and Young

The Voice of Their Hearts: Learning Animal Communication

Remembering the Magick: Fairy Tales for Those Lost, Found, or Wandering

By Salt Water: Tales of the Sea

Spirit Whispers: A Collection of Ghostly Fairy Tales

Yes, I Knit Blankets for Squirrels: A Fairy Tale Author and Her Bushy-Tailed Friends

Not All Witches Are Cruel, Not All Fairy Princesses Are Kind: A Collection of Witch Fairy Tales

Being Different: A Guide for Young Empathic Mediums

Lore from Lavender Lane: Woodland Fairy Tales

The Briar, the Bramble, and the Rose

The Pilgrimage: A Collection of Soul Tales

Nantucket: The True North of My Heart

For my dear friend in China, who risks so much to save the lives of innocent dogs. Words will never be enough to thank her for saving Ruby and Rusty.

And for all the students in China reading my fairy tales because of her......and dreaming of their own happily ever afters.

Table of Contents

Prologue

Where do I begin? So much has changed. I guess the best place to begin is the ending, the ending of my first book, *Birdsong, Barks, and Banter*.

I have been writing this book in my head for a long time now, but never putting it to paper. Perhaps the memories are too painful of those I have lost. I realized that only a few birds are still alive; all my furry friends of those chapters in my life have now crossed into spirit.

Much worse, four of them crossed over very close to each other in time. That time was especially hurtful on my heart, as one loss is quite unbearable enough. I remember a time my veterinarian warned me that many of my dogs were close in age. He said a time would come of heartbreak—he was partially right. The heartbreak was there, but the age was not relevant.

I lost a few long before their time; the monsters of cancer and heart disease chose to take them, despite all the medical intervention we tried. I wrote another book about that grief. It started as a daily blog to journal the path through cancer and disease and grief. It helped my heart; I hope it helped others. I hope one day you will read *Birdsong* and *My Ten Legged Journey*; you will better understand how unique all their personalities were and how each of them came into my life and heart.

So let me begin...along with each tale, memories of blogs I have written over the years will be shared and remembered. Enjoy.

Living with the Pack

Wouldn't it be refreshing to see some ordinary rooms in magazines? It's great to see a vase full of dahlias positioned on a gleaming dining room table, set with polished silver and dainty china. But how about our real lives......

Take yesterday, for instance. I walked into my room to find my exercise bike pedal chewed up, a nice clump missing. Culprit? My collie, Landon.

There are holes in the fringed throws that cover my furniture. There will always be a dust ball of fur floating around the floor......even five minutes after vacuuming. You know how some walls have growth marks for children's heights? My woodwork has chew marks for growing teeth.

Kitchens in magazines......sigh. How could a family of five live there, with not a dish in the drain or a crumb on the counter? Show a kitchen on a rainy day, when dog paws leave a canvas of mud across the floor. Or, show a dog dish with a trail of water puddles left behind by a dripping mouth, leading into the next room.

I imagine that the people who work on these photo shoots must run around like maniacs, preparing the scene. Wouldn't it be nice, though, to just see a *home*, not a show place?

If you own a dog, a cat, or a bird, things will get messy. Let me tell you from experience, birds are the messiest......seeds are flung out of cages, feather dust floats like a fine mist. And if you share your home with all three of these animals, it is pointless to aim for that showplace on the pages of a magazine......but easy to aim for a *home*.

For my home wouldn't be *home* without them—fur, feathers, seeds, chew marks, holes, and most of all, birdsong, barks, and banter.

Love and Loss

I will begin with the cover of *Birdsong*. That picture is of me and my beloved Casper. You couldn't ask for a dog to love you more. There aren't many photos of Casper by himself; he insisted on sticking to me like a furry shadow. His death was one of the worst days of my life. A very aggressive cancer spread into his lungs. I remember him lying down in the vet's office. The vet looked at my face, sensing that I knew. Casper had only lived eight years; it was a week after his ninth birthday. I wish he could have lived much longer, but it never would have been long enough. He will always be by my side, my spirit shadow now.

I also lost Tad and Bram and Bobby; they were my three little Pomeranians. Tad died of old age. Much of his long life was lived in squalor and sorrow, but his old man years were spent in comfort and safety.

Bram succumbed to heart disease. His crossing was the hardest euthanasia I have ever had to decide. He was still looking up at me with that beautiful little fox face in the vet's office. He had acted strange that morning, hiding under a garden bench outside instead of tending to his usual exploration. I noticed on the way to the vet that his tongue had a bluish tint. It was the day before my vet would be away for several days. He told me that Bram might last another day or so, but his end would be difficult and I should let him go while he was still in more comfort than distress. The selfish part of me wanted to grab Bram and run out of the office, seizing each hour of those potential extra two days. But the part that loved him made the choice to euthanize. It was the hardest decision I have ever made, and I made it because I loved him so very much.

Bobby was unique. I called him Bobby S. Mouse. Don't ask me why the *S*; I don't know. *Mouse* because he was tiny and had the cutest little mouse face and bark. Lymphoma attacked his little body. We treated him with chemo, and it seemed to work. Then, a second type of lymphoma, unrelated to the first, decided to invade. This monster was nasty. The tumors were growing so quickly that my little boy's cells were dying. We had no choice but to let him go.

Shortly after Bobby crossed, Easter came. Walking through the pet store, I saw a beautiful little Easter bunny costume. It would have been perfect for my little boy. I bought that costume. The sales clerk at the register made a smiling comment about it; she didn't know my heart was breaking inside. I kept quiet, but I barely made it to my car without tears.

I didn't have my Bobby, but my heart wanted to bring that little bunny suit home. For some hard-to-explain reason, I knew my heart needed to buy it that day. My heart needed a tiny bunny suit that should have adorned my sweet little pom bunny but never would.

It was in that vet's office that I cried each time. Think about it. Who sees you cry so devastatingly besides your family and closest friends? Your vet. He or she is witness to your heart's rawest moments, when all shields break down.

The drive home from the vet's office after my Casper crossed—with an empty back seat in the car—was devastating. I looked up through the windshield and saw the shape of a beautiful, white feather in the clouds. My beautiful white collie was beside me, just up a bit higher in the sky.

How Do You Fill the Empty Places in Your Heart?

How does one fill the empty places in one's heart? You bring home a giant.

It's hard to believe I once held Aura Lea in my lap. She is an Irish Wolfhound. I once measured her tail against my leg......they were the same length. She tips the scale midway between one and two hundred pounds.

I have always loved Irish Wolfhounds. I have a photo of one taped on my refrigerator. There aren't many around, and breeders are extremely selective about prospective buyers for their puppies.

When I took a trip to Ireland and made friends with Oscar, a gentle giant of a wolfhound who lived in a castle, the deal was sealed. I came home and started searching. The first connection didn't materialize, and neither did the second; the litter was not big enough to give me the promised one. And so, my search continued to Virginia, where I found Aura Lea. Her father was from Ireland—maybe he lived in a castle, too.

Aura Lea came home during Christmastime eight years ago. She is named after a Civil War-era love song, sung by both the Northern and Southern soldiers. The tune of Aura Lea would later be used as the melody for Elvis' hit "Love Me Tender."

We are very lucky. I have read some true horror stories of the destruction these dogs can do. For example, I have seen pictures of entire sofas torn apart. The only bad thing Aura Lea did as a puppy was chew a couple of dog beds. The other calamities are not her fault. You learn pretty quickly not to have any knick knacks around on coffee tables when you have a wolfhound. One swish of that tail and it's over. You also don't want to leave a sandwich or cookie out on the kitchen counter when a wolfhound's head is eye level to it. Aura's favorites are Linzer Tarts. I can't say I blame her; they are delicious.

People warned me not to get a wolfhound with tiny dogs. But, as you will later read, that notion was a fallacy. She and Poppy, my tiny, silver toy poodle, were like Big Me and Mini Me.

If you wish to live with a wolfhound, there are some things you must know. First, the sofa will never be your own again. Second, they are sloppy drinkers; they are actually known as "wet beards" in Ireland, for their furry beards are always soaked. And they like to wipe those beards on your lap......regularly. Lastly, they are stubborn and loyal and big babies. My Aura Lea locks herself in the bathroom at the first strike of thunder.

So, if you wish to let into your heart a giant who loves tenderly, choose a wolfhound. (And get yourself an extra lounge chair, for you will never have the sofa to yourself again.)

There is one thing all wolfhound lovers dread, and that is time. Aura Lea is already considered elderly. Gentle giants don't live long; if you're lucky, you might share a decade, sometimes a bit longer. Sadly, when the time comes, that empty place within your heart will be huge.

I Remember......

Aura Lea had the back of our SUV for our three hour road trips to Gettysburg. She was a good traveler, and we never had any issues taking her.

One memorable day, our SUV had serious engine trouble. We could not drive it to a safe place; we barely managed to pull onto the side of the highway.

Terror started racing though my mind of us walking on the shoulder with one very large wolfhound in tow. We called for help, and a trooper came. He looked in the car and said, "I'm not taking THAT." I certainly wasn't leaving her, and the trooper said we couldn't stay there. So, we called a towing service.

The tow truck driver needed to hoist our SUV onto the flatbed of the tow truck. I said, "I am staying inside with Aura Lea." He told me it was illegal; I had to sit in the tow truck, and she had to stay inside the SUV.

My husband and I (in quite the state of panic) climbed in the front of the truck with the driver and watched our beloved Aura Lea being hoisted behind us. I feared she would become frightened and agitated. This is the dog who locks herself in the bathroom if a firecracker goes off down the block.

We watched as she moved her body close to the front seat and positioned her head out the driver's window. It looked like she was driving the car! I imagined the faces of passersby staring up at the SUV with a wolfhound at the wheel. She "drove" the vehicle like a champ.

We made it safely to the garage and waited for my son-in-law to rescue all of us. I think I was more frazzled than she was; in fact, I think she rather enjoyed the adventure.

Here is the blog I wrote the following day:

"Take It Easy…Aura Lea in a Flatbed Tow Truck"

Well, I wasn't on the corner in Winslow, Arizona, but I was on busy Highway 78, Allentown, Pennsylvania. I heard words of dread after a sudden noise from our engine……"It's bad." *You don't want to break down anywhere, but on busy, tractor trailer laden 78, 2 hours from home, with an Irish Wolfhound in the back seat……well, you can imagine.*

My book signing wasn't too eventful. I wore my lucky elephant bracelet, but the crummy weather brought only one reader out to purchase my book. Thankfully, my elephant brought us luck in another, more important way.

The Pennsylvania trooper came quickly. He took one look at Aura Lea in the back seat and said, "You can't stay on this highway, but I cannot fit that dog in my car." *I had already told my husband that there was no way I was leaving her……no way.*

The flatbed tow truck arrived minutes after. I protested, but the tow truck operator said no humans were allowed on the flatbed. Aura would have to ride in our car alone, hoisted on the flatbed. So, I watched Aura Lea being hoisted onto the bed while my heart sank into my stomach.

It turns out she was the calmer of the two of us. Looking back from the cab of the operator's vehicle, I turned 'round to see her head positioned at the driver's seat. I know there must be at least one cell phone photo of it floating around the Internet. I can imagine someone's shock, riding by and seeing a wolfhound posed behind the wheel of a car on a flatbed tow truck!! Then, she calmly lay down in the back seat, enjoying the ride, while her mom sat at the very edge of her seat.

When the tow truck operator handed my husband his business card, I smiled. The logo was...an elephant. Totems will watch over you. (You might have read in one of my previous books about my son-in-law's accident and the large billboard of an elephant looming overhead, watching and protecting his life.)

As you can see, Aura Lea makes herself comfortable in the back seat.

Poppy

Poppy was a rescue. She was old when I adopted her, partially blind, and her bladder did not work very well. Maybe I should say it worked *too* well because we had a lot of cleanups in the house. I fell in love with her photo; she looked like a mini wolfhound, and I needed a tiny dog to cuddle again.

She had terrible skin issues (for which she was being treated) and was finally ready to come home on Mother's Day Sunday. Though partially blind, she adjusted well to the house and got around nicely. She wasn't much of a cuddler, but she did follow me around everywhere, and we shared a wonderful year together.

She and Aura Lea became buddies. That first Halloween, I dressed them both as bumblebees. Poppy had a whole selection of costumes, my favorite being Carmen Miranda, complete with a fruit-laden hat. Poppy truly became Aura Lea's Mini Me (or shall I say Mini *Bee*), and Aura Lea never once let out a whisper of a growl to her miniature friend.

Things took a drastic turn for the worse during the next twelve months. Poppy's blindness got much worse, and so did her bladder issues. She had to be diapered all the time. Poppy could not be groomed without being sedated. I took her to the most experienced groomers, but I would get sorrowful phone calls to pick her up, the task not accomplished or attempted.

My fondest memory is a bittersweet one. We had dropped Poppy off at a reputable groomer in town. I was so hopeful; I had been doing her grooming, but she was getting harder and harder for me to control. The groomer said that Poppy was so stressed out that she was afraid Poppy would die of a heart attack on the table. She requested that I come pick her up. I remember that Poppy, who had never really cuddled or kissed me before, licked my arm when I picked her up. She couldn't see me, but she showed me she felt comfort in my arms, and that made me very happy.

Poppy would get lost in the yard, especially in the snow. She would get stuck behind the refrigerator or in the space behind our computer table. She ventured into the tiniest of spaces, which made freeing her difficult. We had to start blocking off everything. Now, you might think crating would have helped, but Poppy had severe issues with crating. She could not be confined to any space; she must have had a terrible life before she came to our home.

In time, her hearing failed, and she developed canine dementia. This and her advanced blindness made for a bad combination. She would circle and circle and circle in the room nonstop. Then, she started having night terrors. She would bang into walls and appliances and scream during the night. It got so bad that my other dogs started to suffer physically from the stress of watching and hearing her. My vet told us it was time, and we let her go to peace.

I named her Poppy for remembrance of all those whom I had lost. Now, she is also remembered as one of them. I am glad we gave her one short year of happiness. The photos of her smiling face did not reveal the sorrow that would punctuate her future.

When we returned home from the veterinarian, I found my cockatiel Buttons deceased on the bottom of his cage. If you read *Birdsong*, you know his story. Perhaps the two of them journeyed together that day—a little, blind dog and a bird who showed the ultimate sacrifice in forgiveness for what he had done in life.

This little poodle was the impetus for my later adoption of two other little poodles, and for this, I will always be thankful. My little Poppy battled such a war......a war of fear, illness, and confusion. Memories of her are always bittersweet—a mixture of her beautiful smile and bewildered eyes.

Poppy in her happier days

I Remember......

"A Flower's Thirst: Living with Poppy's Cushing's Disease"
(A Funny Tale)

Poppy, our little rescued toy poodle, has Cushing's. This makes her have an incessant thirst for water. This also poses a dilemma in our house. She is partially blind, but she has a homing device for water built inside her......she can search it out better than a pair of dowsing rods. No matter if I change the bowl position each day, she finds it better than Sherlock Holmes could.

Living with other pack members, one of whom is an Irish Wolfhound, means that the dogs' water bowl is about the size of a trough. And Poppy would love nothing more than to sit at that trough and drink herself into oblivion. I know—my little Cairn terrier also had Cushing's. When she went outside in the rain, every puddle, every downspout was her feast.

Yesterday, my husband walked into our bathroom and witnessed a scene that (I would wager) no other dog owner has been privy to. Our pedestal sink's elbow pipe had developed a tiny, slightly larger than a pinprick, hole. A tiny geyser of water was spurting in the air like Old Faithful. Positioned at the stream end was one very open little toy poodle's mouth. Thanksgiving came a bit early; it was a water feast!

Believe me, I couldn't begin to make this stuff up......

Another year passed.......my Queen Bee is now 3, and my tiny bumblebee is in a world of severe dementia and blindness and now gets stuck in weird places, like in my TV cabinet the other night. When I first brought the tiny bumblebee home, she and Aura Lea became fast friends. Now, Aura Lea tolerates this tiny dog—Poppy is always stumbling into her, stumbling on top of her, stumbling everywhere, wondering where her friend has "gone".

Time flies for a wolfhound......three years in a life that is short, even in dog terms. Time has no meaning for a tiny poodle trapped in a senile world of darkness. She gets stuck in places now; we have had to block off the back of our refrigerator, the back of our computer with all the wires.......if there is a nook to fit inside, Poppy will find it.

So today, this blog is dedicated to bees and time......

Both are fleeting......

My two bumbles......one, an especially large species.

Poppy Miranda

Landon

Casper was my Sun; Landon is my Moon

I Remember......

Those of you who follow my writings know how rough these past months have been. In the span of little over a year, I have had to hold the heads of four beloved pets as the final needle entered their suffering bodies. I lost them all to the ravages of illness, three long before their time was due.

When Casper left, he took the sun. He took the light in my heart, the laughter in my day. Then, along came a little poodle who shone a candle back inside my heart, bringing only the joy animals can bring to me.

Now, a little boy with a crescent moon on his back has brought me the moon—the beacon of light that shines to brighten our darkness. He is a gift, a gift from the heavens where all brightness originates. A gift from the spirit of a faithful, beloved friend who knew his love could never be replaced, but strengthened. (All energy is never extinguished—it is only strengthened in another place, filled with love and light.)

The crescent moon on Landon's back

As I write these very words this morning, my Landon turns six months old. Losing Casper was such a loss. I longed for another collie, but I knew I could never replace my beautiful, white collie.

I decided not to replace him. I started looking for a little sable and white collie to fill the emptiness. Again, I searched breeders and rescues and came upon one woman in New Jersey who had a litter of collie pups.

The breeding name was Enchanted. As an author of fairy tales, I took that as a sign. (I later wrote a book entitled <u>Enchanted</u>*). As is usually the case, I went there expecting to pick another boy from the litter. But then the breeder said, "Why don't you hold this one?" Well, "this one" decided to rest his head on my shoulder and take a nap. And he has been napping in my house ever since.*

He isn't Casper; I tried to stop the inevitable comparisons when I brought him home. He was a sable boy, with a crescent moon shape below his neck on his back. Hence, his full name is Landon, Clair de Lune (Landon, Light of the Moon).

Landon is a puppy who never grew up. Casper had not the slightest interest in toys or playing fetch; Landon lives for someone to throw one of his many toys. Landon is gentle; he is a peacemaker who tries to referee the squabbles his little poodle siblings sometimes exhibit. And Landon barks. Now, Casper barked, too; all collies do. However, Landon will bark at nothing, just to make his presence known to the neighbors, whether it is six in the morning or twelve midnight. And if you tell him to stop, he barks louder. Usually, it's a shouting match between me yelling "Landon" and Landon not listening in the least.

Landon found a playmate in Aura Lea. They love to run in the yard. Aura Lea doesn't have the affinity for toys that her brother has, so there are never sharing issues between them......except on the couch, where it is not unusual to see both of them squished together for the premium space.

Landon likes to herd. We often send him outside to round up our wayward poodles. He takes his mission quite seriously.

I Remember……

"I Fell Asleep as Shirl Knobloch and Awoke as June Lockhart"

This morning, 6:30 a.m., I came downstairs to a Lassie episode. Landon was racing through the house, first barking at me, then at my husband. This wasn't just barking "hello." *This was* "I'm stuck in a well" *barking. I was like June Lockhart asking,* "What is it, girl……er, boy?"

This persisted for a few minutes……frenzied barking, running to me, running to the bathtub, running to my husband, more frenzied barking. My husband turned to me and said, "Landon closed the door on himself last night. He was stuck in the bathroom."

Landon likes to lie on the bathroom floor; I guess the cold tile feels good, and if ever there was a place for stinky smells to linger……Anyway, the trauma must have intensified because yesterday was bath day. Ah, I have a collie stuck in a well……er, bathroom.

Signed, June

Landon in the tub—he could happily stand outside in the drenching rain, but what a sad expression when he has some soap and water put on him in the tub!

I Remember......

Readers familiar with my book Birdsong, Barks, and Banter *will know Bailey, my alien pom. Bailey has been under vet care for the past several months; I had suspected a heart issue, but the vet thought otherwise. Allergies were thought to be the problem, and medicine was prescribed. I still wasn't satisfied and pushed for further tests. As it turns out, Bailey's heart and lungs are strong, and that is a blessing.*

Oxygen is what Bailey is having a hard time bringing to his heart and lungs. He has an intrathorasic collapsing trachea. It is a degenerative condition. Degenerative—that's a word you don't want to hear in the vet's office. But the reality of it is, we are all degenerating with each breath.

As fate would have it, it was a tumor (that burst inside his spleen) that took my Bailey. He had gone blind months before, and the vet hadn't suspected the cause to be cancer invading his brain. He would have episodes of being in his own world. The vet told me it was just the adjustment to his darkened world, but it wasn't the blindness—it was cancer, ravaging his body and eventually exploding, causing him to bleed internally very quickly.

I know that around the rings of Saturn spans a rainbow-colored bridge. Even aliens have to go home one day. My little alien pom had to return home. When he arrived, I hope he told the others about a crazy Earth lady who loved him in spite of all his antics.

I think they have sent another down from the mother ship anyway.......Landon, Light of the Moon, my collie puppy. A song from The Sound of Music *always plays in my head with Landon. He isn't running across the Alps, but he is running into constant trouble. Remember the song?* "How do you solve a problem like Maria...How do you hold a moonbeam in your hand?" *I got his middle name right.*

Landon likes to chew things. His fifty stuffed toys aren't enough; he is always searching for the fifty-first. I have a lot of soft sculpture things about the house. (I already wrote about the Bethany Lowe Easter Bunny that had a serious mishap this past spring.) My Halloween pumpkins and witches were a problem. Where could I display them, other than hanging them from the ceiling? I decided to tie them against the stair railing leading to the second floor. Safe, right?

Yesterday, I walked into the living room. Landon had climbed the stairs and was standing on his hind paws, front paws perched over the banister, looking down at me. He had a witch nose in his mouth. Yes, I guess Landon would be at home in the Alps......he likes to climb, too!

Bailey and Landon, my two bad boys......each breath of my life wouldn't be the same without them.

Buddy and Bailey were my two models; I could dress them in anything. I loved Halloween with these two.

Bailey as Shrek...his costume is on backwards!

Buddy as Shrek

The Easter Buddy!

LANDON
Shirl Knobloch ©

I Remember......

"A Message from Another Planet"

I have been waiting for Bailey to contact me after he crossed. He is an alien, after all—why should the mere lines of dimension stop him from saying hello?

Then, it happened......at 1:20 last night, it came. The loud crash......Landon barking his head off......

My clock on my living room wall fell, the nail still in the wall slanting downward. On the tumble down, the clock broke all but one of my hummingbird figurines. The only one left untouched was a music box that plays:

> Que sera, sera,
>
> Whatever will be, will be
>
> The future's not ours to see
>
> Que sera, sera

I love hummingbirds. My dear friend JBee (who crossed several years ago) did, too. She left me a hummingbird pin in her will. Could she be telling me my little alien had crossed into a new realm, still causing trouble? Oh, what antics she is in store for......

Thanks for the sign, my friend. Next time, could you make it a bit more peaceful?

Ah, the fragility of life......the future's not ours to see......

Here are the fragments of the broken figurines I could collect; the rest are behind a TV cabinet that has to be moved. The music box is in the upper left-hand corner, untouched.

I love my hummingbird statues. Now, they are only shells, as bodies always were. My husband glued all the statues......they have peacefully sat on the shelf since then. If only we could repair our loved ones' broken bodies, too, and have them sit beside us once more.

I Remember……

*It was approximately five o'clock in the morning. Landon, our collie baby, started barking nonstop. A couple of shouts of "*Landon*" did nothing to stop him, so I told my husband he'd better investigate. Landon doesn't bark like that at night. I was in a semi sleep/wake state, dreaming of my collie Casper who left me this past April.*

My husband got up, went downstairs, and saw an agitated collie barking and jumping about in his crate. Aura Lea, my wolfhound, was minding her own business, wondering what the to-do was all about. My husband heard some strange sounds coming from the back of the house in our sunroom. (We have a sunroom designed to be an addition to our kitchen space, but now it has become the rescue spot for trees. I have several live Norfolk pines from Christmases past, as well as a towering ficus, a huge, ceiling-height plant that was rescued from the garbage at the office I worked at over a decade ago.)

Amidst the trees, our small, blind poodle, Poppy, was trapped, her paw nails clicking against all the huge clay pots as she vainly tried to find her way out of the Amazon rain forest. I have no doubts—had he not been crated, that baby collie of mine would have done some herding in the dark. Poppy was rounded up, and Landon was quiet......that is, until his 6 a.m. wake up pee call.

I gave Landon a big thank you hug and went upstairs. I also whispered a thank you to Casper, who I know was also watching over. He had come to me in my dream to tell me so.

My pack......rarely a quiet moment. At least we have Lassie on patrol and a collie spirit guardian to save us from the "wells of life" and rescue our little, blind lamb.

I Remember......

I raise doves, and I feed wild ones. Each day for one week, a very sick dove came to my door. She walked in circles, stumbled over at times, and had only enough strength to fly in short spurts when I attempted to come too close. As days passed, I would get closer, within inches, but she would still attempt an escape flight.

Yesterday morning, she did not come. I went out to run errands, and upon returning home, I found her still body; she was lying on her side at the end of my driveway near the gutter. My husband saw her and avoided crushing her body with his tires. I got out, wanting to retrieve her remains to bury her at peace. She was still alive. She slept peacefully, the strength of her body slowly ebbing. Her death was coming, but she would not be under the wheels of a passing car or in the grasp of a hungry predator.

I lost my Poppy in April. We had rescued her, nearly blind and deaf, two years prior. After one year, she began to suffer from severe neurological issues. She walked in endless circles, stumbled over, and no longer knew day from night (being blind and deaf). Nighttime episodes of her tiny body thrashing against walls or into appliances became too much for her and us to endure. Euthanizing her was one of my hardest decisions. She would still eat if led to a bowl, though she lost the use of her hind legs at the very end. The vet said it was time, and my intelligent mind knew it was time, but she was my first decision for one who was not dying. She was *dying—she was suffering—but not like those before who had cancer and heart disease. She was dying in a different kind of way.*

I have had a very difficult time these past months. But as I watched a little dove circle aimlessly, stumble over, and become unable to walk, I saw what granting a peaceful crossing means. It can mean putting a little poodle to rest who is not able to settle herself into calm existence, or it can mean picking up a tired body from the curb to breathe her final breaths in serenity.

Gifts from spirit come in many forms. I believe this dying dove came to me for a reason; she was a gift—a gift from Poppy to perhaps say, "Thank you."

Buddy

If you read *Birdsong*, you know that a gentle nurse named Buddy (also known as Clara Barton) was part of my family. Buddy took six months to utter a bark; he had been so badly frightened in his puppy days. I won't go into his whole story here, but Buddy traveled from a kill shelter in Virginia to find his way into my heart and home.

Buddy was a black dog. It mystifies me how people pass by black dogs in shelters; they are the last to be adopted. My gentle, caring Buddy might never have had a chance at life if my son hadn't picked this frightened, silent dog who cowered in the corner.

Bud had long, thin legs. (He might have been part Doberman, though we never knew his lineage. He was just the perfect mix of love and kindness.) Cancer developed in Bud's leg. Those skinny legs didn't give our vet much to graft together in surgery, but he did an exceptional job, and Buddy lived for a year.

The vet said that if this type of cancer did not return after six months, the coast was pretty clear. But another cancer developed. This one was an aggressive anal sac cancer. There wasn't much that could be done except give Bud the best final months that he so very much deserved.

I read some disturbing symptoms that might be waiting in his future. Bud's cancer decided to take a route to his brain. In the twelve years of his life (we can only estimate his age), Buddy had never had a seizure. Seizures are frightening; I have been Mom to several little poodles who had seizures. A big dog having a seizure is even more terrifying to watch. One morning, I came into the kitchen to find my Bud in his own little world in front of our dishwasher. He was clearly in another place; he wasn't convulsing, but his brain was in a deep, faraway place. It is hard to explain, but this type of seizure was even more disturbing than the frenetic movements of the other type with which I had been so familiar. The vet said this wasn't good news and this would only escalate.

Again, like with my Bram, I had a very, very difficult decision ahead of me. In the periods between seizures, Bud was fine. But Bud was such an exceptional boy, he deserved to cross in peace and dignity, like the gentleman he truly was—and we gave him that crossing. I held him and told him what a good boy he was. I know Florence Nightingale had an owl at her shoulder, so maybe Clara Barton has a Buddy by her side now, nursing those in need.

The morning after Buddy crossed, I woke up to find a beautiful little rainbow on my bedroom ceiling. I hadn't placed any new crystals or suncatchers at the window or sill to reflect this prism. I haven't seen it since. It just appeared for a little while that morning. I think it was the Universe telling me that a kind and gentle soul was at peace.

When you search those rescue sites or roam the halls of a dog shelter, remember—under black fur might beat the heart of a rainbow.

I Remember......

"Yoga with Bud"

Bud is my yoga partner. His siblings are too rambunctious and therefore banished to another room. Bud, however, lies beside my yoga mat, teddy bear gently clasped in his mouth, practicing his own meditative routine.

Usually, the teddy bear is stolen by Landon. During these brief morning moments, though, Bud has dominion over the toy bin and can peacefully lower his stress, raise his comfort level, and feel grounded to his space. Isn't that the purpose of yoga? Some do it on a mat......some only need a teddy bear.

I Remember......

"Don't Leave a Dog Alone in a Room with a Starfish"

I had a slight panic attack yesterday. I was showing my grandson a couple of my dried starfish; he loves the star shape. I placed them on a low table in the living room, and we went to play some PBS computer games in the den.

About 45 minutes later, I walked into the living room. The starfish were gone! I looked on the floor. Nothing. Not an arm or leg......except those of the black dog that skulked guiltily out of the room. Maybe it was retaliation. After all, Bud is subjected to some humiliating photographs......

PANIC*! I Googled,* "Do dogs eat starfish?" *To my amazement, countless posts sprang up.* Help me, my Chihuahua ate a fist-sized starfish......help me, my greyhound ate a bowl of starfish at my rental home......*and so on. Evidently, the saltiness and fishy taste are quite tempting to dogs. Who would have imagined it?*

***RELIEF**. Most replies commented that the dog would survive. Maybe there would be some vomiting and diarrhea, or some difficulty passing stool (if the spiky arms and legs were "stuck" on the way out).*

*Some starfish, the article stated further, contain neurotoxins......seizures and nerve damage could result. **PANIC AGAIN**!*

The article said that as long as the starfish came from local waters, the dog should be safe. How would I know where my starfish came from?????? I wasn't in the mood for a starfish communication session from beyond, although I did feel sorry that its desiccated, little body had to be abused that way.

Bud (the skulker) never chews, so I anticipated some spikes "coming out." The advice was to feed the dog pumpkin (to provide fiber to ease the journey), so my huge can of pumpkin was opened and administered. Bud is okay. Some bits of starfish pieces and loose stools this morning.

Now, I guess I'll bake a pumpkin pie for Spring Equinox with the rest of that huge can waiting in my fridge. Nothing heralds in spring like a pumpkin pie......

That's it...... ***I am NEVER leaving a dog alone in a room with a starfish again.***

Side note: It's only right that my Clara Barton, nurse to my pack, should become nursemaid to ailing dogs around the globe. This blog post has garnered the most worldwide views of my postings. People from all across the world, in panic mode, come to my page (and my Bud) when their dogs ingest these spiky sea creatures. Even in spirit, my Bud continues to be a source of kindness and help to those in need. His gentle soul cannot be dimmed by death.

Buddy and His Teddy Bear

I Remember......

"Living with a Bunch of Furry Kids"

Anyone who lives with a pack of dogs knows they are just like kids. They get jealous over toys, they get jealous over beds, they can be spiteful, and they can be so compassionate your heart will melt.

We have a toy bin......yes, a toy bin of stuffed and chew toys. We have a collie puppy. He must first empty the bin (every single time) before he chooses the one he wants. Of course, the others make their selections, too. I find toys hidden in their favorite corners, like pirate doubloons. They make "dibs" over beds and blankets, too. It reminds me of shotgun......who calls it first, gets it.

This is Bud. He is a shepherd, perhaps rottie, perhaps dobie, perhaps anything mix. He tips the scale at a rather portly number, but he likes to sleep in my toy poodle's bed. Like I said, a bunch of jealous kids fighting over who gets the favorite toy or a favorite bed that is way too small for him.

(As you can see in the picture, his selection of toys is nearby.)

Smokey

You read about my James Dean in *Birdsong*. Smokey was only a few years old when my father-in-law died. We promised him that we would care for Smokey when the time came, and we kept that promise for over a decade, until Smokey joined him once again.

We gave Smokey the best life we could. He suffered from seizures and had medical issues. The years took their toll in the end; his vision failed, and he moved with the debilitating pain of joint issues.

Smokey wasn't the easiest. For example, it was a nightmare to clip his nails; the whole town probably thought some torture was occurring at my house. (Smokey had the very vocal voice of a Shiba Inu, and he wasn't afraid to use it.) But, he grew on you. Sometimes, you would find his face just staring at you, wondering how and why he now had to live in this house filled with annoying siblings. He wanted to be the one and only dog, as he had been for my father-in-law. I know my father-in-law was just waiting to take him home and make him King of the Castle again.

Smokey liked to play with bricks……yes, you read that right. Now, I had a toy poodle who liked to play fetch with rocks. Once, when I took her to the vet, the vet remarked on the "state" of her teeth. What could I say? I couldn't stop this dog from picking up rocks on the ground and wanting you to throw them. She was obsessed. I loved her, but she had her puppy mill emotional residue issues.

But back to the bricks……Smokey was strong. He once tunneled his way under the snow from one end of my father-in-law's yard to the other! So, carrying a brick around in his mouth was no big deal. When Smokey came to live with us, we took a few bricks from my father-in-law's yard. Smokey never picked one up again. I guess he knew……

A youthful Smokey

My very elderly Smokey

China

One of the most incredible journeys of my life began this past December 15, 2018. That was the day I met two little dogs who have since changed my life. I have been loving and rescuing dogs for most of my life......since reading *The Incredible Journey* as a child. *The Incredible Journey* is the story of a quest to find home, a long and arduous journey traveled by two dogs and a cat, facing miles and miles between them and safety.

But now, back to December 15......I had read a story about Debi Kruse of Precious Petz Rescue in Warwick, New York. She rescued poodles from China. I had lost my little poodle rescue Poppy a couple of years earlier. She was old and almost totally blind when I adopted her and brought her home on Mother's Day. She lived two years before becoming very ill. I shared my home with gentle giants—a collie, a wolfhound, and one with a mixture of unknown parentage (what most would call a mutt). But, my heart longed to hold a tiny dog in my arms and heart again. Debi posted a photo of a gentle, chocolate-colored poodle, and what I can only call Divine Providence set its magic to work.

My daughter lives near Warwick. I was going to be traveling there for my grandson's birthday party. I wrote to Debi and asked if I could come see the girl. We arrived to find the shy, gentle girl the rescue had named Ruby. Her name in China had been Arya. She was a meat trade breeding dog. Her age was about five, since that is the age most meat breeding dogs are sold to the slaughterhouse. Arya was heading to the slaughterhouse when a kind Chinese rescuer saved her life.

Then, Debi brought in a bundle of red-furred energy named Meng Meng, who had arrived from China only the night before. The rescue had renamed him Rusty. He immediately planted himself at my feet, belly up, tail wagging, longing for all my attention and heart. "I think he's chosen you," said Debi.

Meng Meng is about the same age as Ruby. He had a home in China, but he had become ill and was in need of surgery. Unfortunately, some people view medical needs as imperfections and abandon pets because of them. That same Chinese rescuer gave Meng Meng his chance at lifesaving surgery. Without this savior, Meng Meng would have met a horrendous fate of possible beatings or being sent to the slaughterhouse. Many dogs in China are kidnapped from the streets for the meat trade; my tiny Meng Meng didn't stand a chance.

I think Debi was pretty astounded when I announced that we'd be taking both home that night. My heart felt that Rusty wanted me and that Ruby needed me. Hence, I made one of the best decisions of my life.

There were worries. How would Ruby and Rusty adjust? Would my own dogs get along with them? My worries instantly faded as these two little travelers walked inside my house like they had lived there all their lives. There was no adjustment period; the sofa became theirs, the house became theirs, and my yard became theirs in which to run and play.

Then, through the wonders of social media, I saw a Chinese woman holding a dog who looked remarkably like Rusty. I wrote to her and asked if she was indeed the one who had saved him. I learned that, in fact, she had saved *both* Rusty and Ruby. She is a teacher in China and a devoted animal rescuer. She loved Meng Meng, but her circumstances in life did not permit her to keep him. So, she enabled Debi to oversee his journey to America.

Yue Tang and I have become fast friends. I told her that she will always be Rusty's Chinese mom, and I his American one.

She has given my heart two very precious gifts......and a third gift, as well, in her friendship. We talked about my writing and my books, and I asked if she would like me to send her some.

The journey of those books has become even more incredible. Tang is a teacher, and she is using them in her classroom, helping her students improve their English and inspiring them to have compassion for all animals. Tang teaches at an all-girls school; its motto is *Independence, Ability, Care, and Elegance*. Tang hopes these girls will one day spread light into the dark corners of Chinese traditions that many are trying to change.

Yes, the cruelty of the meat trade is abhorrent. But there is cruelty in all corners of the globe. Not all Chinese people believe in this tradition; there are many who are rescuing and enlightening others to seek a compassionate way of life. In Tang's words, "Many volunteers are going there to teach children of the village people! Breeding dogs and slaughter houses are all typical of those places! China is a huge forest."

I am so proud to have my books play a small role in nurturing that forest of kindness. Perhaps my words will reach into the hearts of those girls and kindle love and compassion.

Sometimes, you find friendship next door. Sometimes, you find friendship across the globe. I am so fortunate to have found both. Two little furry ambassadors are now spreading kindness in a way I never would have imagined, and a dear human friend continues her mission of love on the other side of the world.

I am sending my second shipment of books to her today. Included in the box are bookmarks featuring pictures of Rusty and Ruby. These two little poodles have changed my world......maybe they will change the world across the globe, too, for others waiting to begin their own incredible journeys.

Rusty (on the left) and Ruby (on the right)

Rusty makes quite a handsome gingerbread man!

Ruby with her pretty purple flower

I Remember......

Ruby is my miniature poodle. She is about five years old, the age when Chinese meat farm breeders find less use for their "cash cows" and sell them to the slaughterhouse. Ruby was rescued on her way to that slaughterhouse. Devoted angels on both sides of the sea enabled me to rescue her, along with her poodle brother, Rusty, who was rescued from the streets of Shanghai.

One morning, I found a few of my paperback books in my dogs' toy chest. Strange? Perhaps. But I have a poodle named Ruby who likes to "take" stuff......usually in the early morning hours. Sometimes, it's my knitting. One time, it was my scissors......thankfully, no injury was sustained.

This morning, I found my reading glasses lying in her dog bed. So, mystery solved—I have a poodle who reads during the night......

Ruby's "Book of the Month" selections are, as follows......

<u>Blind Hope, a Dog and the Woman She Rescued</u>

<u>Nantucket Ghost Stories</u>

<u>The Pig Who Sang to the Moon</u>

Eclectic taste......just like her mom.

Ruby never knew life outside her cage, never held a toy in her paws. Now, she delights in collecting them. She collects her own, those of her siblings, and those of visiting canine relatives who must relinquish all stuffed toys to her.

By day, Ruby sits by my side on the sofa while I read or knit. By night, my reading glasses, my entire knitted piece, a skein of wool, or just a few strands of yarn make their way to the sofa. Maybe it's Ruby's hoard. I have read accounts of trauma survivors who become hoarders. Captain George Pollard of the whaling ship "Essex" *was discovered to have hoarded food in his Nantucket attic. Depression era survivors always had a well-stocked pantry, just in case......*

How can I be angry at Ruby for being a thief in the night? Perhaps the darkness of night heightens fears that she will once again face the cruelty of her past. When she first came to me, she flinched at every move my hand made to reach down and pet her fearful body. Now, there are still moments when, caught red handed, she looks at me with fear in her eyes.......fear that I will act with cruelty and harm, not with love and understanding.

I love Ruby. I smile when I see my reading glasses and yarn on the sofa. Maybe it is her way of making sure there will be a tomorrow, one with her sitting on the sofa next to someone knitting or reading—or just loving her.

I Remember......

"Mornings of Mischief"

They work as a team. Aura Lea, my Irish Wolfhound, swishes her tail and knocks my reading glasses off the living room end table. Ruby, my poodle, then carries them into her bed.

My knitting needle and yarn are strewn across the rug......now with a thousand collie fur strands attached to it. A home without them is no home for me......

I gather up their breakfast bowls. They each have their designated place; I carry Ruby's into the living room as I hear Rusty, my other poodle, darting toward the kitchen.

Rusty sits upon my kitchen chair and starts to eat. He just started doing this and now claims his place at the table each day for breakfast and dinner. I have had him a little more than a month now; when he came, he seemed to be apprehensive of any dog bowl I put out for him. I literally had to sit with him and either hand feed him each bite or drop individual bites on the floor—then he would eat. (Rusty and Ruby came from China. What they faced is unimaginable to most people living in countries where dogs are not thought of as food.) When no bowl worked, I decided to try one of my grandson's Kermit saucers. He liked it! Watching him sit at the kitchen table, eating from his Kermit dish, one would never suspect the horrible world Rusty escaped from a little over a month ago.

Okay, I know it's not the best in dog manners. But such simple pleasures—a few minutes at the table eating from a Kermit bowl or thievery of glasses and yarn—are priceless. Such small things to replace such tremendous horrors left behind forever.

Now, my two little poodles and their co-conspirators in crime fill my days with mischief and joy in being free. They fill my heart each day with love. It's unimaginable to me how they might have filled one's plate with dinner......

Here is Rusty eating from his Kermit dish.

I Remember......

"Teaching Rusty the Ropes...or, How Poodles Become Collies"

Collies like to bark. You learn that the hard way, usually when you are standing at the door in your robe and pajamas in the early morning and you are screaming for the barking to stop. You can try to train, try to be the dominant one, bribe with cookies—all efforts are futile. For a collie must release his song to the world at all times......especially in the very early morning or very late at night.

A collie needs only the air to bark. Why wait to find something at which to voice the alarm? Voice it first and tell every squirrel, bird, or human within a block radius that you have arrived. No matter that your mom is screaming at the door to be quiet—that just makes sounding the alarm more pertinent at the moment.

Now, little Rusty is following his big brother's lead. The minute his tiny paws step over the door threshold, his poodle song is released. My poodle barks the song of all those still trapped in fear and abuse. He sings the glorious song of freedom......his "Collie/Poodle" bark.

Now, his only fear is of a raindrop falling on his head. (Rusty doesn't like the rain.) Landon, on the other hand, loves it; he will stand out in the drenching downpour, not a care in the world. I keep hoping some of that will rub off on Rusty, too; it is almost an impossible endeavor to get him to go out in the rain. But, a world where rain is the enemy is such a better place than the world from which he journeyed three years before. His little bark—part Collie, part Chinese, part Knobloch pack now—is loud and clear and safe......and that is a glorious song.

Living with Mice

Having a Civil War farmhouse has introduced me to the world of mice. Wild mice that creep into the abundant holes and crevices to find warmth and shelter. But, several years ago, I brought home a little pet shop mouse that soon crept into the crevices of my heart.

Blaze

I named him Blaze. A blaze is the white streak that the breeders of Lassie looked for in each dog that portrayed the canine hero. Collies with this blaze are especially prized, though I think they are all beautiful. Blaze had a black body with a distinctive white streak on his head. His fur was long and silky; he was quite a handsome gent.

Each night at bedtime, he would get a piece of a Ritz cracker. I always kept his room—yes, he had a room which he shared with a few bird buddies—dark at night. (Birds and small animals do best when their body rhythms are in tune with nature's clock.) In the dark, I would call him—yes, mice do respond to your voice. He would wait patiently and reach out his paw or tiny mouth gently to grasp this delicious treat. We did this every night; like nature's clock, Blaze waited for his cookie.

He was spoiled; he would munch on grated carrots and lettuce and vegetables, along with the seeds he loved. At Christmas, I hung a little stocking in his cage, which he enjoyed climbing and investigating, tunneling inside for treats.

I watched Blaze get old before my eyes. One day, he started walking like an old man. He was only two. I cried the day I found him motionless. I realized how a tiny mouse could sneak inside your heart forever.

I Remember......

"A Heart from a Little Mouse"

It all depends on how you look at things......

Now, most will see a chewed up toilet tissue roll.

Me, I see a heart.

I see a thank you for all his special cookie treats. A thank you for his morning songs. A thank you for saving his life when I watched other mice beating up on him in the pet store cage.

So, I see a heart. I don't need to see one; he has my heart anyway. Still, seeing one gladdens mine......

It all depends on how you look at things. Those things can change your day.

Sometimes, a little mouse can make a big difference......

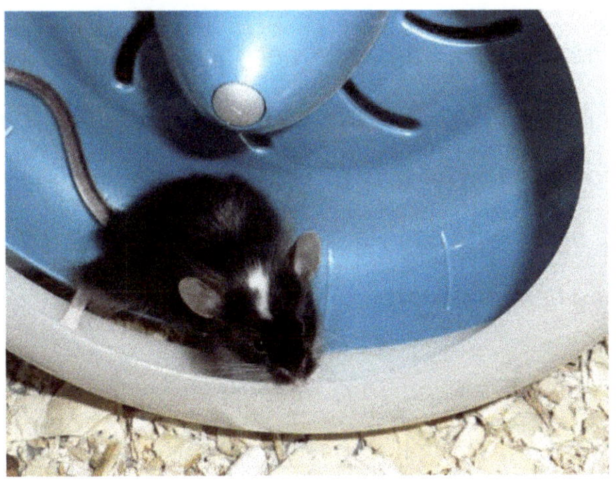

I Remember......

"Lessons from a Tiny Mouse"

My mouse died during the night. I watched him suddenly grow old this past week. I could literally see him become an old man before my eyes. I guess time speeds up for a tiny mouse. Mine lived two years, the normal life span of a pet mouse. In the wild, a mouse has so many dangers to face that I guess two years is a miracle.

I learned in those two years how special it is to love a mouse—and that it is possible for a mouse to "love" me. He waited each morning for his tiny crumb of cookie, right up to yesterday, when he struggled and fell back three times trying to reach for that crumb. I knew he was dying, but his will to live paralleled any man's.

I think a mouse is a wonderful pet for a child. In two years, that child learns love, care, and acceptance of life's fragility. I learned how wonderful it is to share not only one's home but also one's heart with such a tiny being—one who leaves such emptiness when he departs.

I think everyone reading this, at least everyone with a child, will remember the book If You Give a Mouse a Cookie. *I would like to amend that book's last pages......if you give a mouse a cookie, he will steal your heart.*

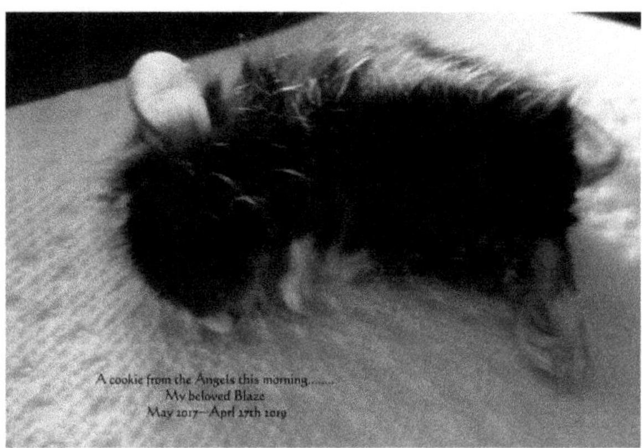

Angels are waiting, my little boy, with all your favorite cookie crumbs.

Mr. Bumbles

When Blaze was about one, I decided it would be a nice idea to get him a friend. Mr. Bumbles was grey; he looked like a little mouse you might find trespassing in your basement. He soon became my second spoiled boy.

I went to the pet shop and asked the worker to capture the one I had selected—a tiny, grey boy acting rambunctiously in the glass tank. The pet shop worker, annoyed, went to the tank and hurriedly picked up the first mouse she could, one acting very quietly in the corner. She angrily said, "What does it matter? You're only going to feed him to a snake." I was so distraught at this and told her this was to be my pet. Immediately, her expression softened, and she said, "No wonder you were being choosy." Now, this wasn't the one I had chosen, but I was so upset—and knew I could love any one of them—that I took him home.

I named him Mr. Bumbles. He was so tiny! As it turned out, Blaze did not want any company in his palace of a cage; I could see the look in his eye that this tiny baby would be in trouble. Mice can be very cruel; they can fight to the death. I put Mr. Bumbles in his own cage. I was right about thinking there was something wrong in his quiet nature; he didn't act like a mouse should. He died soon after.

I wrote this blog after he crossed:

Mr. Bumbles crossed peacefully into spirit during the night. I brought him home from the pet store on Sunday. The pet store worker was very nasty to me. I asked for a certain mouse, and she said, "What difference does it make? I don't have all day for you to pick one out......you just want him for food anyway." *Mr. Bumbles wasn't the mouse I chose—she hastily grabbed Mr. Bumbles by the tail—but it didn't matter. The one caught was the one meant to come home that afternoon......*

No, I didn't want him for food. Unfortunately, these tiny beings are bred in horrendous conditions, born to be somebody's meal and that's all. For less than the price of a fancy coffee, you can bring one home and choose his fate. More often than not, they are in poor health. Some can bear the stress of being shipped to pet stores and then to another strange home......some cannot. Mr. Bumbles could not.

To be loved or eaten—that is their awaiting destiny.......

To be loved or eaten......I choose love.

At least he died in the darkness of night, in peace, with someone who cared to mourn the loss of his life when the sun rose. His eyes were closed in peaceful slumber, not staring fearfully into a predator's eyes, waiting to snatch his breath. Maybe he was chosen for just that reason—so that he could die peacefully in his nest in a safe place. All my life, old and sick ones have come to me to cross in peace......

Rest in peace, Mr. Bumbles. Your life meant something to me......and you will always be loved.

The Tale of Miss Charlotte Bumbles

Those who read my blogs know I brought home a baby mouse this past weekend. He only lived one full day and peacefully crossed during the night. I named him Mr. Bumbles, in remembrance of a dear friend whose birthday it was that Sunday.

Heartbroken, I wondered if I should get another, especially since the pet store worker had been especially nasty to me. As a result, my husband drove me to a more distant pet shop to find another mouse to comfort my heart and fill the new cage that sat forlornly empty.

When we arrived, the pet display cases had signs stating, "New ones coming soon." *So, my husband drove me even further away to another store. (I didn't want to meet that nasty worker again at the shop close to me, and I didn't want to bring home another baby from that same litter who might carry similar illness.)*

We walked to the small animal display case and saw a bunch of white mice sleeping, huddled in their plastic cave......while one light brown one reached her paws on the glass to greet me. Her breathing was very heavy. Living with animals all my adult life, I worried about this......it wasn't a good sign. I sat there, watching her and worrying about bringing her home and facing the same heartbreak as the days before.

Finally, after about twenty minutes, she retired to sleep, still breathing very hard. I said to my husband, "I can't keep taking the sick ones. It is too hard on my own heart."

So, we walked to the car. I said, "Don't go. Let's just sit here for a while." *My husband turned and said,* "Are we going back in???"

We went back in. My husband got the worker and asked about my mouse. I voiced my concerns about her health. He said it might be stress. He also mentioned that a little black and white mouse was sold the day before......she was the only different *one now. Perhaps the bunch of white ones were bullying her......*

That was it......she came home. She is thankfully doing well, enjoying a bunch of good food and a peaceful cage. I named her Charlotte because she climbs and jumps like Spiderman, and her acrobatic moves remind me of a spider weaving her web. Thus, Charlotte (from Charlotte's Web, *one of my favorite stories) seemed appropriate. Like Spiderman, she crawls upside down on the cage roof, dangling on one leg......*

I hope she is well......if not, then my heart will pay the price. By now, I should realize that I have a long-standing account with the old and sick ones, forever making withdrawals from my heart but collecting deposits that are priceless in return.

Miss Charlotte Bumbles lived about 8 months. She had a fancy two-tier cage with a little compartment in which I would always put special treats.

Like Blaze, we had our cookie ritual. Miss Charlotte would wait in the dark and reach out her paw for her Ritz at the corner of that special compartment. I would enter the room in the dark, call out her name, and she would run to her spot to collect her treat.

One night, her paw didn't reach. My heart sank. I retrieved a flashlight and shone it into her cage. She was lying on her side, with one paw holding onto the wire rung. My pretty girl had left me.

I haven't gotten another mouse since. I try to avoid pet shop mouse tanks; my heart would be tempted to bring one home again. Mice are very intelligent and mischievous little characters. They require a lot of care, but their very tiny hearts will show you love in return.

My little ones are all buried in my yard. A stone mouse statue holding a rose adorns the spot. Each time I sit nearby, I remember the little mice who stole my heart in their short time as part of my family.

I Remember......

"Tell the Angels—One Cookie in the Morning, One Before Bed"

My little mouse, Miss Charlotte Bumbles, crossed last night. She was fine yesterday; she ate, she played, she came to greet me with her ever smiling face.

I went in to give her her bedtime cookie, but no whiskered face greeted me at the cage door......I knew.

Such a gentle girl......

Such a short life......

Such an everlasting sorrow in my heart......

I think she has a smile on her face. It was hopefully a peaceful death, what she deserved.

Tell the Angels......one cookie in the morning, and one before bed.

I Remember......

"Advice to Mouse Moms and Dads—Always Check the Wheel"

If you read my blogs, you know I have a pet mouse. Having a mouse has made me realize what intelligence these tiny beings possess. Each morning, my Blaze comes to the rungs of his cage and sticks out his tiny nose and mouse paws at this strange creature singing Good Morning to him. Okay......it's for the corn muffin or pancake treat (that accompanies his morning vegetable or fruit) that he does this.

The one worry of any mouse owner is of their potential escape. Blaze's cage needs to be cleaned every couple of days; mice have their own particular "aroma." It can be quite pungent, to put it nicely. I call him stinky.

Anyway, after years of caring for small beings, like dwarf hamsters, I came up with a pretty good method, which I thought was foolproof......until this morning. I have a large plastic bin that I put Blaze's entire cage inside. I remove the cage top, letting him out to roam the bin (which he cannot climb out of). Then, I remove and clean the cage bottom. The clean bottom is lowered back into the bin, careful not to squash mouse feet or other personal parts. When he climbs inside, I attach the top on again. Easy, right?

Well, today, my husband (who was helping me—cleaning a mouse cage is a two-human procedure) did just so. He put the entire cage into the bin and detached the top, giving Blaze a chance to climb out. As he placed the cage top on the table, I looked in the bin and asked alarmingly, "Where's the mouse!?!"

Blaze had been in his wheel when my husband, unknowingly, lifted him about five feet off the ground to place the cage top on the table. Now, Blaze was ***out of*** *the wheel and leisurely roaming the top of my table, chewing on the tablecloth.*

How could we safely get Blaze back into the large plastic bin? That was our problem. "Wait," *I shouted as my husband attempted to slide the bottom of the cage under the top.* "Let's think about this." *A mouse can sneak through the tiniest of openings; I was fearful Blaze would escape and run right off the table.* "I know," *I proceeded.* "I will place his corn muffin crumb in the wheel. He will go back inside, and then you can quickly slide on the bottom."

Well, Blaze had other ideas. He decided he was going to place only his head in the wheel to eat—his bottom and paws were firmly planted on the tablecloth.

"Let me get a cup," *I suggested. My dwarf hamsters always climbed in cups. Blaze, however, wasn't having any part of the cup trickery.*

Finally, after five minutes of stress, we got him safely inside, where he happily commenced chewing on his muffin crumb.

My advice to all mouse owners? Always check the wheel......

My Baby Jay

Last year, a baby blue jay chose our stair railing to be his place of rest. He lingered for quite a while, and at first, I thought it best just to let him be. When he refused to move and our dogs were getting a bit too interested, we decided to take him in.

I was torn about doing that. A lot of times their parents are watching from afar, just letting them have room to spread their wings. Later that evening, my husband gently placed him in the bushes in our backyard. We hoped for the best—that his parents would find him.

That night, about midnight, my husband opened the back door to let our dogs out one last time. There, on the same place on the railing, sat the baby jay. That was enough for me. We brought him in. Luckily, in my house there is always a spare cage or two, or three, or four......

The baby thrived for a couple of weeks. He ate, he flew about my back sunroom, and he wandered across my bookshelves; we loved him. He would soon be released to live his life in the sky.

One sad morning, however, he was lying on the floor of the cage. My husband found him when he woke up to take the dogs out. We never understood why. He had eaten the night before, and he seemed to be fine.

His passing will always be one of the saddest memories of my years of rescue. Should I have left him outside? My friends say there must have been something wrong for him to return to that railing that night.

I hope he has found the sky he so longingly looked for in this picture. This is one of the last poignant ones I took of him.

Deciding which book to read

Sneezy

Two springs ago, a baby starling hopped into my life. He was sick; he sneezed all the time with some sort of respiratory ailment. I took him in, cared for him, and raised him back to health. I tried calling him all sorts of names that would fit such a beautiful bird—black gemstone names, mythical being names. But the only name that stuck was Sneezy. Even when he stopped sneezing, it was too late. He would always be my Sneezy.

We tried setting Sneezy free twice. When the first attempt failed and he returned, I can't honestly say that my heart wasn't happy. I had grown attached to him. Still, I wanted to give him back the sky. We tried a second time, and when this one failed, I knew he was mine.

Sneezy, I later found out, is a girl. It's hard to tell the gender of birds, but starlings have a difference in the color that surrounds their pupils. She loves to take baths, and her favorite foods are chopped, fresh herbs. (Starling nutritional needs are very important, and their diets must provide the proper foods for their health.)

Sneezy talks up a storm! She knows all of my dogs' names; when I take the dogs out, I often hear her call out, "Rusty, Ruby" or "Let's go." She loves to chatter throughout the day, and she loves to listen to music.

I cannot imagine my life without the song and words of a starling. Most think of them as pests, but I can tell you they are extraordinary beings of this earth. I love them so much that I wrote a fairy tale about how they got their stars.

Harry Potter and Dobby

One trip to the pet store brought two babies home.

Harry Potter was a little brindle mouse. (The last one I became Mom to several years ago had the cutest striped fur and most handsome set of ears.)

Dobby is a skinny pig, a hairless guinea pig that sat languishing in her cage because people thought she was ugly. I thought she was quite lovely. She looks like a tiny hippo with a soft tuft of fur on her head. The salesgirl said I could have her for the sale price; she didn't know I would have gladly paid full price for her. The shop just wanted to be rid of this ugly thing that nobody thought was cute enough to buy.

Buy them both, I did.

Harry lived under two years. Most pet shop mice barely make it to two years old. Poor breeding usually causes a host of health issues. Dobby is still with me, celebrating her third, maybe closer to fourth, birthday. (I don't know how long she sat in the shop before I brought her home.)

Dobby is a queen. She eats organic vegetables and herbs. Since she has not fur, she has to eat constantly in order to regulate her body temperature. She has her morning hay and guinea pig food, which she rarely eats because she is spoiled with fresh fruits, vegetables, and herbs. Then mid morning, her tray of assorted veggies, herbs, and fruits is served with more hay. An afternoon snack consists of more veggies, herbs, fruits, and hay. Nighttime is still more hay and a guinea pig treat, which she waits for like clockwork. We always say in our house that the one who eats best is Dobby.

She is very gentle and loving, and I'm so glad she came home with me to receive the care she needs and deserves. Sometimes, I wonder what would have happened if she went to a home that didn't provide all the things she needs. She probably wouldn't be alive today.

That day at the pet shop was the best two-for-one sale I ever found. Harry now rests with Blaze, Mr. Bumbles, and Charlotte in my yard.

A Gift from the Heavens

I end with the tale of my two doves, mated for almost two decades in my home. I tell the story of how they were abandoned in *Birdsong*.

They were the most devoted pair of birds, helping me raise other rescues as their own. Over the years, they lost several malformed, unhealthy babies of their own. Perhaps that is the reason they were abandoned; they weren't money makers for breeders.

During the pandemic, the male dove died. I think his mate still looks for him.

A couple of days ago, a beautiful dove flew to my doorstep. She remained there all day. She wasn't like the wild mourning doves. I could tell she was tame. I could stand very close to her and talk; she wasn't skittish around humans.

Perhaps she escaped from a breeder, or perhaps she was released at a wedding ceremony. (By the way, this is something you should never consider. Those doves rarely fare well out in the wild.) She stayed all day and flew off somewhere unseen late in the afternoon.

The next morning, she returned. She seemed lost. The wild doves would not mingle with her. She sat alone in a low branch of my tree, listening to me talk to her all day long as I passed.

Late that afternoon, I made the decision to see if she would come to our outstretched hands. She did, and we placed her inside one of my cages. She was not stressed in the least; she seems so content in our home. The dogs' barking doesn't even faze her! She settled in as if this were her home for years. My grandson named her Marshmallow, and she fills my house with grateful coos.

I believe she was a gift for all the years of care and love I have given to doves. She somehow found her way to my home, where love and food and shelter were waiting. I have been a dove keeper for decades. When my male died, I resolved that soon, with the passing of his mate, the cooing of doves would no longer grace my home. Now, this gift has given me precious song to fill my home once again, for however long the Universe allows. However old she is, her remaining years will be filled with comfort and safety and love.

Epilogue
The Light Continues

Early this morning, when I awoke and came downstairs, a beautiful beam of morning sunlight was focused on a photograph of me and my Little Guy. I think it was St. Lucy's light, telling me that Little Guy was in her arms......

I raced for my camera and turned it on, but the charge was dead. I guess some things will not be "captured." Some things must be believed, like faith and St. Lucy.

St. Lucy is the saint of light. Today is her Feast Day (December 13). In that very dark room, sunlight filtered in and brightened my heart and day. When the day comes, and a beautiful beam of light appears at the end of a tunnel, it is my heart's wish that Little Guy and all the others will be waiting.

I hope you have enjoyed this journey to revisit those most precious in my life. Thank you, and please consider reading *Birdsong, Barks, and Banter* to learn more about those mentioned in this book and all the others who paved my path of rescue and love.

Wishing you Light, and remember—when one song ends, another begins.

Somewhere, sometime, in years ahead......I hope someone will pick up one of my books in some thrift store or antique shop (hopefully they will still be around), smile, and bring a part of me—and a part of all those whom I loved—home. –Shirl

www.ingramcontent.com/pod-product-compliance
Ingram Content Group UK Ltd.
Pitfield, Milton Keynes, MK11 3LW, UK
UKHW021332070726
13610UKWH00011B/36

9 798218 042332